SOMETHING FOR THE KIDS

Fifty-Two Children's Sermons
for Worship

TED LAZICKI

MERIWETHER PUBLISHING LTD.
COLORADO SPRINGS, COLORADO

Meriwether Publishing Ltd., Publisher
P.O. Box 7710
Colorado Springs, CO 80933

Executive Editor: Arthur Zapel
Manuscript Editor: Kathy Pijanowski
Cover and Inside Design: Michelle Z. Gallardo

Library of Congress Cataloging-in-Publication Data

Lazicki, Ted.
    Something for the kids.
    1. Children's sermons.   I. Title.
BV4315.L34   1985   252'.0413   85-62468
ISBN 0-916260-34-8

66 *Children are a heritage from the Lord — blessed is the man whose quiver is full of them.* **99**

—*Psalm 127: 3-4*

*To my six children and sixteen
grandchildren, who have caused me
to experience the wonderful truth
of these words, I joyfully dedicate
this book. I pray that thousands
who hear these stories told might also
come to know and serve our
wonderful Saviour.*

TABLE OF CONTENTS

III. SIN

IV. HOLIDAYS AND SPECIAL USE

INTRODUCTION

What's in it for me? Have your children ever asked this question as they were being pushed, dragged, coaxed or coerced into church on a Sunday morning?

They may never have used those words, but I suspect that there are few children who have not asked that question on some occasion.

You may have considered that the answer should have been self-evident to them, and not replied. Or you may have resorted to that answer born of age-old parental frustration — "Because I said so." Now lest anyone think I have never had to face this, I hasten to add that I have had six normal children (four of whom, incidentally, are in full-time Christian service), who at various times exhibited some very normal foot-dragging on Sunday mornings. And I suspect that there were times when "because I said so" was the only answer they got. But consider: How long would you attend services if there was virtually nothing at your level of interest or understanding, and it was obvious that no effort was being made to provide it?

Since most Christians have their first meeting with Jesus before their teens, we should wonder why we don't see the folly of spending 85 percent of the church's time, energy and concern on the adults, who have for the most part already made their life's commitment, and the remaining 15 percent on the children, whose eternal destiny is yet unsure.

A pastor friend of mine was attending, with his family, a church close by their vacation spot. Driving back home on Sunday evening, he asked his kids how they liked the church. *"Lots better than ours"* was the verdict. Well, this called for a hard question: *"Why?"*.

"Because they had something for the kids."

---

* Throughout this book, the words *he, him* and *his* are intended to mean also *she, her* and *hers,* to include all people, regardless of sex.

They had a story for the children at every Sunday morning 11 o'clock service. I trust it goes without saying that that daddy has not let a single morning service go by since that time without a story for the children — *something for the kids.*

A son-in-law of mine was serving a church in Minnesota a few years ago. As many have done from time to time, he prepared a questionnaire in which he asked the congregation to rate every phase of the church's program. On a scale of one to ten, they were to rate each activity's worth, effectiveness and need for improvement; or the advisability of eliminating it.

Lives there a pastor with pride so dead who would not have naturally expected his Sunday morning sermons to be number one? It was humbling to find that this did not happen. First place went to the children's stories he told each Sunday morning. When he was later about to leave for another place of ministry, the one stipulation his former congregation set for a new pastor was that he must have a story time for the children.

Since you have purchased this book, I can assume you either have a story time or are willing to give it a try. Following are some suggestions that can make the time easier and more effective:

- Forget the adults that are there. Take no note of them. Don't do or say anything in any way different because they are there. If you can't let your hair down, if your dignity is going to be a factor, turn the job over to somebody else.

- Bring the children to the front and have them sit in the first pews or on the platform. Involve them as much as possible in the story, asking and answering questions, helping with any object lessons or stories.

- Occasionally use another person and make it a dialogue. My son and his wife are a team. I usually have my grandson work with me.

- Develop your own stories. Make them as personal as possible. Use names, places and people with which the children are familiar. I once had in my Sunday school class a young man with a serious psychological problem. He sat with his head down, looking into his lap the entire time. It was only when I related a personal experience that he looked at me.

To say, "Once there was a girl who . . ." or "I heard about a man once who . . ." is not half so effective as when you, or someone the children know, or an object or association with which they are familiar, is mentioned. Strive, within the bounds of truth, to make your stories about real people, the ones they know.

- Don't hesitate to start, and continue even though you have but a few children attending. You will have as many eavesdroppers as you have adults in the building. You will never be able to speak to the adults more simply or directly than you can with your stories for the children. Every congregation has those adults who turn off their hearing whenever the sermon touches a sensitive area in their lives, something they are protecting. They sit with their armor in place. However, their defenses are down during the children's story because "it's only for the kids."

- My son's church bulletin lists this time as "For Children Only." Everyone in the congregation must consider himself/herself in this category, since eyes and ears are riveted to the front pew during this time slot. Don't insist that children beyond the sixth grade come forward. They are usually hesitant to be with the "little kids." They will get the message from where they are.

- If you have never done this before, the hardest part is getting started, especially developing your own stories. But as you launch out, you will find coming to you Bible passsages, everyday encounters, incidents from your past and from that of friends which make excellent story-sermons.

- Ideally, these can be based on the sermon text for the day, but I suggest you do not start here. I have tried this and know how difficult some texts can be. You will not want to become discouraged.

- Don't be afraid to use as much humor as possible. Obviously, you can't turn this time into a circus, but if all your children have to look forward to on Sunday morning is boredom, we are all in trouble.

● If this is going to be a new feature in your morning service, you obviously are going to have to find a time slot for it. If you strive to keep a tight schedule, then something is going to have to be cut out or shortened. This is a good question to ask: If this service is going to have any long-term effect on the lives of our children, will the message more likely come from our children's story or, for example, one of the hymns that may have to be eliminated to make time?

Try this: Select an unfamiliar hymn to be sung during the service. At the close of the service, ask those to raise their hands who could tell you the message of that hymn. Next, ask for a show of hands of those who could tell you the message of the children's story. Leave out a hymn? I am only suggesting that the church give the children the priority they deserve.

● *Don't* read your story! No matter how well you can express yourself when doing so, the message reading sends is, "It's not important enough to me to take the time to memorize it." But it *is* important.

● While these stories were written primarily to assist those churches which do not have a junior church during their morning service, they can be used just as well for junior church services and for the opening service of Sunday school.

● Many of these were written for use by a particular church, and of course, names and situations will need to be changed to fit your group. I left them as they were originally written to show how they can, and should be, very personal. Put in your personality, your people, your foibles.

● Try putting a provocative title in the church bulletin, and give a hint about next Sunday's story. These little touches capture the children's interest and make it evident they are important.

If ever Jesus' words, "Allow the children to come to me," are needed in the church's program today, it is, strangely enough, in the morning worship service.

So for children young and old, I offer the stories that follow. How I wish it were possible for me to slip in some Sunday morning and listen as these, or even better, those which you have developed, are told. If you feel any of your stories should have wider circulation, you might like to send them along to Meriwether Publishing Ltd., giving permission to include them in a future edition.

Bless you as you become a blessing to the little ones whom Jesus loves so much.

WHAT GOD
DOES FOR US

#1

LOOK WHO SENT ME A LETTER*

God's Love

(As you begin this, have several pieces of mail in your hand, and look at each one for a few moments.)
Good morning.

Do you kids like to get mail? A lot depends on *whom* it's from and *what's* in it, doesn't it? Some of the mail your mom and dad get they surely don't like. *(Pretend to open an envelope, looking at contents with a sick look on your face.)* *Bills!* We sure don't like them, do we?

But then there is Valentine's Day. That's fun. Especially when somebody sends you a box of candy. Or at Christmas time — did you ever get a Christmas card with a green piece of paper tucked inside . . . and on the corner of that green piece of paper was a big number five? Wow! A five-dollar bill!

Suppose you came home from school one day and your mom said, "There's a letter for you." Would you say, "Ah, just put it down somewhere. I'll read it sometime if I feel like it."? Oh, no! You would grab it and open it right away, wouldn't you?

When you get older, someone will probably send you a love letter. Do you know what a love letter is? Yes, it's a letter from one person in love, to the person with whom he's in love. Do you think anybody ignores a love letter? Just puts it aside and doesn't read it? Oh, no! As soon as he sees whom it's from, he tears open the envelope. *(Pretend to open an envelope quickly and read it. Move your head from side to side. When you're finished, look up and sigh audibly.)*

What would you think of somebody who got a lot of love letters from someone and never even bothered to read them? You don't think that could happen? It does, *all the time.* The most wonderful love letters ever written are not read by most of the people to whom they are sent. Can you guess who wrote them? That's right — God did. All of the books in the New Testament are God's love letters to you. Wouldn't it be a terrible thing not to read some of them every day?

* II Corinthians 3:2

You don't have to wait for the mail truck. You don't need to wonder if there is something for you, because there always is, every day. You don't need to worry about bills, because Jesus paid it all — what he gives us is *free*.

#2
WOW, WHAT A BARGAIN!*
Everlasting Life

I've got a riddle for you this morning. Listen very carefully. Suppose you walked by a toy store and saw a sign that said, "Six-dollar-and-fifty-cent slot cars only forty-five cents." Or you saw ten-dollar dolls for only one dollar. Or even suppose you went by *(name of a popular local department store)* _____ and saw fifty women just fighting to get inside because there was a big sign that said, "Big sale — seventy-five percent off on everything."

Now what's one word that describes all these situations? I'll give you a little hint. It starts with a *B*. *(If this is not enough of a hint, give them one letter at a time.)*

Right! A *bargain*! Everybody loves a bargain. Do you know what a bargain is? That's right. When you get something that's very good or very expensive for very little, that's a bargain. Every time your parents go to the store, they hunt for bargains.

Now what was the biggest bargain anyone ever got? *(Don't wait for an answer.)* Let me give you some clues. You can't see it or pay for it. You can read about it in a book, and people have told you about it many times. The bargain is for a limited time only. It's just like when your mom says, "Oh, I should have taken advantage of that sale at *(store's name)* _____ , but now it's too late."

It's the same way with this bargain — millions of people have waited too long. Millions of people don't realize what a bargain they are missing, and millions of people all over the world have never even heard about it. Because they haven't heard, and because it is so wonderful, lots of people leave home and travel to the farthest corners of the

* **II Corinthians 8:9**

world to tell them.

Now, what is this bargain? That's right, God saw how bad this world was and that he could never take people to heaven the way they were. So he said, "Because I love them, I'm going to give them my son, Jesus. If they will ask him to, he will take their sins — the bad things they do — and give them everlasting life in heaven." Now, isn't that the best bargain anyone ever had?

But remember, don't wait. No one knows when God will close the door, and it will be forever too late.

<h1 style="text-align:center">#3</h1>

IT'S GREAT TO BE ADOPTED*

God's Love

(If there is anyone in the acquaintance of some member of the congregation to whom this can apply, use his or her name. This story was originally written about my son and daughter-in-law, who adopted a four-year-old named Tisha, so I have used her name.)

This morning, we are going to tell you a story about a little four-year-old girl named Tisha.

Do you know what it means to adopt a baby? Well, sometimes when people don't have children of their own, they take into their home a little baby or a little child whose real mommy and daddy couldn't take care of it. This baby then becomes theirs. This is called adopting. This is what happened to a man named Dan and his wife Judy. Now when they found out they could have Tisha, they drove down to the county office, took her by the hand and led her out to their car.

Now do you suppose when she got in the car they said, "Now, Tisha, this isn't really *your* car, because you are only adopted."? Or when they got to their house, they said, "Now, this is not really your house, Tisha; you're only adopted."?

No sirree! They said, "This is *your* car, because you are *our* little girl; we've adopted you! This is *your* home, this

* **Ephesians 1:3-8**

is *your* bedroom, that's *your* bed, those are *your* toys. You are *our* little girl, because we have adopted you. Do you see that refrigerator and those cupboards and that food? They're *yours,* because we've adopted you! Everything in this house is yours."

Do you know that a lot of people in this room are adopted? *(Name four or five Christians present who are known to the children.)* They are all adopted. Do you know who adopted them? God did! Many, many years ago, God looked down on this earth and saw how bad people were and that they were all lost, and he could never let them into his heaven that way, or they would spoil it. So he said: I'm going to send my Son, Jesus, down to earth. He will die for them. And if they will admit how bad they are and ask him to forgive them, then I will adopt them into my family, and they can come to my house in heaven and live with me *forever.* No one who isn't adopted by God will ever get to heaven.

If you are not sure that God has adopted you, ask your mom or dad or your Sunday school teacher, and one of them will tell you how you can be sure.

#4

I CAN'T; THAT'S IMPOSSIBLE*

God's Healing

Good morning.

Let's talk this morning about doing something that's impossible, shall we? Can you think of anything that's impossible to do?

What does it mean to do something that's impossible? You know, doing something *that can't be done. (Mention several things to which the children, depending on their ages, can relate.)*

Well, let me give you a for-instance. Once when Jesus was in the temple, some people brought in a man whose hand was crumpled up. *(Bend your right arm and wrist up sharply and hold them in this position until you reach the*

* **Matthew 12:10-14**

appropriate point in the story.)

Now, the man needed to be healed; he needed to be able to work to buy food for his family. But Jesus said a strange thing to him. Jesus told him to stretch out his hand, but he couldn't do that — it was impossible. If he could, he wouldn't be there — he wouldn't need to be healed. Why did Jesus tell this man to do something that was impossible? Jesus knew it was not possible for that man to do it. He had probably tried many times.

But the man did it. Now, what made it possible? *Yes,* we can *always* do what Jesus tells us to — even when it seems impossible.

All through your life, you are going to read or hear about things from which God wants you to stay away, that other people are doing. You are going to think, "It's too hard; it's *impossible.*" Anything God wants you to do, Jesus will help you do, even if it seems impossible at first.

#5

WHO SAID IT BEST?*

Love

Let's have a little contest today, shall we? Who do you think will win?

First, I want you to tell me what the three most wonderful words in the English language are. *(Should some sharp kids say, "Father, Son and Holy Spirit," you'll have to change your contest to "the second most." Pause.)* I love you — right. You win the first part.

Now, the second part gets harder. How many ways can you say *I love you*? That's correct — with your mouth is one way — to your mom or dad; especially to your grandma. When you do, it makes her feel so good, she could just *burst.*

Someday, you boys are going to tell your special sweetheart that, and she'll be so happy, she'll turn pink. Oh, yes, you will, you'll see, and I hope it's a girl God picks out for you. But is there a way to say *I love you* besides just with your mouth? *(Pause.)* Can your hands say *I love you*? *(Give*

* **Matthew 5:41**

the children a chance to think of ways.) Sure, by the things we do and make for people. These can say *I love you.* How about your feet? Yes, even your feet can say it. Did you ever think you could have talking feet? In the Bible, it says we should go an extra mile for someone. That means we should go farther than we have to. Love goes an extra mile. When we do that for somebody, it can say *I love you.*

Now here's the last question: Who found the very best way to say *I love you?* God did, didn't he? When did he say it? *(Pause.)* When he gave us Jesus. Jesus is God's "I love you" to each one of us.

#6

I'LL TRADE YOU*

God's Gift

(If there is any chance that any of the younger ones might not understand the concept of trading, the storyteller could do a little pretend trading to illustrate.)

Do you kids ever trade things? You know: I'll trade you my slot car for your knife, or if you'll give me that doll, I'll give you my teddy bear *(or whatever seems likely to the kids there).* Did you ever trade something, and your mom and dad were not happy at all about it? They said, "You go and trade right back." They thought it was not a fair trade; that what you got was not as good as what you traded for it; that what you gave or traded was something that they wanted you to keep, no matter what.

But did you know that you do a lot of trading every day? So do your mom and dad. Your dad and your mom, if she works away from home, trade eight hours' work on the job for a paycheck. That can be a good trade.

When your mom goes to the store, she trades money for that asparagus you like. You don't like asparagus? You'd rather she would trade it for ice cream? OK, I'll tell her.

So you see, kids, it's not bad to trade. Trades are only bad if we get cheated. Let me show you. Now suppose you have been saving your allowance or some money your grandma

* **I Peter 2:24**

gave you for your birthday. You know what you want, and you go to the store and find it on the counter. But the clerk is busy. The devil tells you, "Nobody's looking; just take it and save your money." If you ever did that, you would be making a trade — you would trade your honesty for something for which you didn't pay. That would be a *bad* trade. Or you promised your mom that you would come right home from school. But your friend said, "Ah, come on home with me first. I have something I want to show you." So he did, and you were an hour late. You traded your promise to your mother for a little bit of fun. That was a *bad* trade.

But there are lots of good trades, too. Suppose your mom says, "If you clean up your room really well, I've got something special for you." And you do. That's a good trade. You study real hard and you get a good grade in school — maybe an *A-plus*. That's a good trade.

Do you know who made the most wonderful trade that ever was? Can you think of who got the best bargain ever given? Who gave the least and got the most? We did — every one of us who loves our Lord Jesus. When Jesus went to the cross, he took all our sins and gave us forgiveness. We traded everlasting death for everlasting life. Isn't that a trade you would think everybody would want to make?

#7

BE SURE YOU COME UP HERE*

The Wonder of Heaven

You know, children, the Bible doesn't really tell us much about heaven, does it? I think I know the reason why. Have any of you ever seen a dragonfly? Well, they are about this long *(hold your fingers about two inches apart)*, and they have beautiful wings. They like to fly around water. I'm going to tell you a story about a dragonfly, and then I think you'll understand why God did not tell us more about heaven.

OK, now listen: Once upon a time, beside a beautiful stream that ran through a glorious mountain meadow, lived five ugly brown worms. These worms lived in the mud. They

* **I Corinthians 2:9**

were born in the mud, and all they had ever seen was mud. Now they knew that it would be time soon for the oldest one to wiggle up through the mud to the top, and then live on the outside. They didn't know what it was like out of the mud, but they wondered and wondered about it many times, until finally, they decided that when the oldest one went out, he was to come back and tell them about life on the outside. He promised he would. Soon, the time came, and he wiggled and crawled and poked his nose through to the top, and there he was.

He couldn't believe his eyes! He looked and looked and looked again. Soon, he was pretty tired from all the surprises, so he just fell asleep in the sun. And while he was sleeping, his body changed, and he was no longer an ugly brown worm, but a beautiful dragonfly.

If you kids were ever up in the mountains, you saw how beautiful the dragonflies there are. First, he tried out his wings — *he could fly*! He went skimming over the sparkling stream. He went from one pretty meadow flower to another. He zoomed *(with open palm, show dragonfly zooming)* around all the trees. He watched the white clouds go floating across the blue, blue sky. Everything was so glorious, it almost took his breath away.

Then he said, "Oh, oh, I almost forgot. I promised I would tell my friends what it is like out here." So he quickly flew to the mud bank and sat there on a little pebble and looked at that brown mud. Then he looked at his beautiful, long blue body, his delicate wings, and said, "I can't get back into that mud. Even if I could, how could they understand? How could I tell them how beautiful a sky is when all they have seen is mud?" And so he shouted in dragonfly language, *"Your ears have never heard, your eyes have never seen anything so beautiful, so glorious. Be sure you come up here!"* And then he flew off to skim over the sparkling streams again.

Now do you see why God has not told us more about heaven? We would never be able to understand — it's so wonderful! But he sent prophets and teachers and pastors to tell us: *Be sure you come up here!*

#8

GOD'S WEED-KILLER*

Help through the Bible

Hi, kids!

We are going to have a horticultural story this morning. Boy, doesn't that sound exciting? It doesn't? Well, maybe that's because you don't know the meaning of the word *horticulture*. The dictionary says it means *the science of growing plants*. Now, does it sound exciting? It still doesn't? Well, just listen and maybe you will change your mind.

Now, who can tell me the difference between a weed and a good plant — you know, like flowers, vegetables and trees? They may look alike, but we know they are not, because your mom and dad like the plants, but they sure don't like the weeds. They dig them up, chop them down, and get rid of them any way they can. But how can you tell the two apart? How can you tell what's a weed and what's a plant? Well, there is one way to tell, but your mom probably will never let you try it. Just go out into your garden and trample on everything. *(Show the action.)* Do you know what would happen? Well, first, you'd probably get a spanking; then probably all the plants would die. But do you know what the weeds would do? Just laugh at you and keep on growing. You can't kill weeds that easily.

Do you know what weeds are like? They are like bad habits in your life. It's not easy to get rid of them. It's not enough to say, "Well, I won't do that anymore. I won't talk like that anymore." *(Say these last two sentences with no conviction.)* Those weeds, those habits, will be back the next day. You'll be doing just what you said you wouldn't do.

No, you've got to get mad at your bad habits — just the way your dad gets mad at the weeds. Tell Jesus you need help to get rid of them. And the first time you see one coming back, when you realize you've done or said something you shouldn't, just say, "Jesus, I'm sorry I did — or said — that. But because you're helping me, I'm going to get rid of that weed, *and I mean it.*"

* **Isaiah 55:8-11**

If you go down to the nursery, you can buy lots of weed-killers for your garden, but nothing beats the Bible for a weed-killer in your life. Those bad habits lie down and die if you attack them with God's word — God's weed-killer.

SECTION II

LIFE
AS A CHRISTIAN

#9

LET'S JOIN
THE GREAT RACE*

Being a Christian

Did any of you kids watch the track events on TV in the last Olympics? You know, the running races? They were exciting, weren't they? You saw the runners line up at the start *(lots of excitement in your voice).* They bend over . . . then, *bang!* goes the starting gun, and *they're off* ! Sometimes, they run so hard, they even collapse on the track.

Now, what would you think if you saw somebody in a race who had a TV set on his back . . . or who was too sleepy to run . . . or who stopped to play with somebody on the track . . . or who went so slowly that he finally started to run in the wrong direction? You think that couldn't happen? It happens all the time.

Do you know that each of you kids is in a race right now — even though you're sitting down? So is everybody else in this room — even though they, too, are sitting down. Let me read you something from the Bible. *(Read I Corinthians 9:24-27.)* So you see, we are all in a race, and God says we can be *winners.* Isn't that *great?* God wants us to work, to play, to pray as though being a Christian is the greatest thing in all the world — *and it is. (Say this next sentence seriously and slowly.)* I think each of us knows something God wants him to do. *(Look out over audience.)* So, get on your marks . . . get set . . . go!

#10

THE ONLY LAW WE NEED**

Love

You know, kids, we sure have a lot of laws, don't we? Do you think we need them all? It seems like every day,

* **I Corinthians 9:24-27**
** **Romans 13:10**

somebody makes a new law telling us what we should do or what we shouldn't do. We have laws in school, in our home, when we are driving our cars — everywhere we go, laws, laws, laws. Thousands of them. Don't do this. Don't do that. Don't drive faster than fifty-five miles an hour. Don't run in the hallways. Don't yell when your baby sister is sleeping. Don't lean back in your chair. Don't cheat on your income tax. Why, if you wrote down all the laws we are supposed to obey, the paper would fill this church — and maybe a couple more.

Hmmm. With so many laws, why are there so many people in jail? Why do so many kids get spanked? But, do you know, I just figured something out. We don't *need* all those laws; *we only need one.* That's right, *only one.* Listen; I'm going to show you from the Bible. *(Read Romans 13:10 from* Good News for Modern Man *or* The Living Bible — *these bring it out more clearly.)*

You see, love *is* all the law we need. Now, would you drive too fast if you loved everybody on the highway? If you really loved your little sister, would you tease or hit her? If you loved your teacher, would you do anything to make it hard for her or to make her unhappy? And *(looking at adults)* if you really loved God, wouldn't you want to talk to him every day and read the love letters he wrote to you?

So, you see, love is the only law we need.

#11

WE HAVE TO READ
THE INSTRUCTION BOOK*

The Bible

(You'll need a large manila envelope, containing a large sheet of white paper and another sheet with printing of any nature.)
I saw some people flying paper airplanes the other day. Some really could fly a long way; so I thought I'd try it here this morning. Are you surprised to see a preacher sail

* **Psalm 119:130**

paper airplanes in church? Well, let me do it just this once. I bought a kit from *(name of local store)* _____ . So let's see what we've got. *(Pull out a white sheet.)* Well, here's the airplane, or it will be.

Now let's see how we do it. *(Pull out the instruction sheet. Mumble under your breath.)* First, take paper . . . mumble. . . . Fold in center . . . be sure you . . . mumble . . . take care to . . . measure very carefully. . . . *(Crumple up instructions and drop them.)* Ah, I don't need those. Besides, they are too hard to understand. I can figure it out myself. *(Proceed to fold in various ways until you've got a monstrosity that cannot possibly fly.)*

Well, now, if theirs flew, mine will, too. Here goes! *(Toss it out over the kids' heads.)* Hmmm. Now I wonder why that didn't fly. . . . I tried real hard . . . and it was real good paper. It sure took a nose dive, didn't it?

Now why do you suppose that happened? That's right. I didn't read the instructions. I had them. . . . I can read. . . . They were there for me. Can you think of anything else that takes nose dives? That falls? That fails? That crashes?

Sure, people do. They end up in jail, get hooked on drugs, marry somebody they shouldn't, they flunk in school . . . why? It's easy to see why. They don't read the instruction book. God provided it. . . . Somebody printed it. . . . They know how to read . . . but they just ignored it, just as I did with my paper airplane instructions. Now do you want to escape a lot of nose dives in life? Read the instruction book every day. *(Hold up the Bible.)*

#12

JOINT HEIRS WITH JESUS*

In God's Will

(This story will take a little rewriting to make it applicable to the people telling the story and to one of the children. It is written here as it was originally done, so that you can see its possibilities.)

* **Romans 8:15-17**

Have you ever wished somebody would leave you a lot of money? I'll have to admit I have. What would you *(to one of the kids)* do with a million dollars?

I can think of a lot of things I could do with a million dollars. Maybe one of you has a rich uncle who will leave you a million. You know, I don't really know many rich people, especially any who would leave *me* any money. But if someone does, I'll give you each part of it. That would make us joint heirs. That means we would share equally. We would each get the same amount. The Bible talks about joint heirs.

I'm going to show you all what it means. Now I've got three wills here, and I'm going to give them to three of you children. Do you know what a will is? It's a paper people make out that tells who they want to get their money and property when they die. In these wills, you are joint heirs with someone else in the will. OK, ready?

(Give the first will to someone with a brother or sister; the second and third, to others. Take back the envelope from the first child and say, using his or her name:) _____ , let's see what you get. You are joint heir with your brother *(or sister; insert name)* _____ . "Whereas — whereas — whereas" . . . you get your dad's pickup truck (of course, it will be thirty years old by then), his high school varsity football jersey, and . . . oh . . . his shoulder pads, too. Of course, you have to share them with your brother *(or sister)*.

Let me read your *(to second child)* will. "Whereas — whereas" . . . wow! You are joint heirs with the richest girl in *(your state)* _____ . Let's see what you get: three Cadillacs, an ice cream factory and a lifetime pass to Disneyland.

Now let's see number three. Hmmm. This is the best one of all. We were just kidding about the others, but this one is real. This is absolutely genuine. Because God promised it in his Bible. He signed it. *(Hold up the Bible.)* Here, it says that if you love him, you are joint heirs with Jesus Christ. That means that everything God is giving to Jesus, he is one day going to give to you. Now doesn't that make it worthwhile to live for Jesus?

We know that for some of you younger ones, this is a little hard to understand. I'd be glad to explain it to you sometime, or ask your Sunday school teacher or your mom or dad.

But let's be sure we are *in* God's will so we will *be* joint heirs with Jesus.

#13
WHERE DOES GOD LIVE?*
God's House

Good morning.

Did you kids notice that people act differently in church from the way they do at home or at school? Why do you suppose this is? *(The answer you want is "because this is God's house.")* Oh, because this is God's house. Do we all agree with that? This is God's house? Do you think you are nearer to God here than at school? *(Get answers to all of these questions, but don't respond to them.)* Do you think God is more likely to hear your prayers and answer them if you are praying here? Do you think that God is in our church now? . . . Does he live here? . . . Will he stay here to wait for us to come back next Sunday?

Suppose you were having an argument with a friend as you walked into church. Would you probably stop when you got in the door? . . . Why? Do you come to church to meet God?

I'm going to read you something from the Bible. Listen very carefully to what it says. *(Read Acts 7:48 or 17:24.)* What did that say? Right. If you are a Christian, if you have asked Jesus to forgive you and make you his child, then God's home is in your heart.

Well, if God doesn't live here, why do we come here every Sunday? *Right* — to learn more about him . . . to worship him with others . . . to hear our pastor tell us how we can better know God and serve him. . . . That's why we should come every Sunday.

Where will God be when we leave today? *Right.* He will go right with us. He will be just as close at home, just as close on the playground at school as he is here. Isn't that wonderful?

* **Acts 7:48**

#14

LOOK OUT FOR THAT BIG WAVE*

Eternity

(In this story, you will have to make changes, if any of it is not true for you. Change it from sand castles to Lego™ - block houses, or whatever, but make it personal.)

Have you children ever built sand castles? It's fun, isn't it? I've built some beautiful ones, with towers, a moat, bridges, battlements . . .

I was thinking about these when I was reading my Bible. God's word says we should not work for food that just disappears. Let me read it. *(Read John 6:27.)* What did Jesus mean? Isn't that what your dad works for, so that your family can eat? Sure. Then what is Jesus talking about? Well, it's not food he means. What Jesus is saying is that we should work for something that lasts. Take my sand castle, for instance. I spent *hours* on it, and do you know what? A big wave came and washed it all away — gone, nothing left.

That's true of a lot of things. My glorious sand castle perished in one big *swish*. But there are lots of things that do last — like homework, for instance. Now, I know it's more fun to watch *(popular TV show in your area)* _____ _____ ; but when you turn off the TV, it's gone — just like my sand castle. But with your homework, you can learn something you'll be glad you know and can use sixty years later.

But what God is really talking about is things he wants us to work for that last for eternity — forever! You know, I don't always feel like preparing my sermons *(or Sunday school lessons, etc.)*, or even reading my Bible. That's my homework. If I always did what I felt like, I'd spend a lot of time *(playing golf or tennis or gardening — whatever is true for you)* _____ . But these things, too, will all be gone someday, just like my sand castle. But what you put in your mind and heart — or somebody else's mind and heart — can last forever, and ever, and ever — and that's a long, long time.

* **Matthew 7:24-26**

#15

AW, HE'S JUST A LITTLE SQUIRT*

Worthiness

Good morning, kids.

Before I begin our story, I'd like the biggest boy or girl and the smallest boy or girl to come up here and stand side by side. *(Put them back to back and remark how much taller the larger one is than the smaller.)*

(Name) _____ is a lot bigger than *(other child's name)* _____ , isn't he/she? *(They return to their seats.)* Now, how much difference does it make to God how big or how little we are? *(Wait for an answer.)* It doesn't matter. It's all the same to God, isn't it? He doesn't measure people that way.

I'm going to tell you a story that happened thousands of years ago. The children of Israel had a very bad king named Saul. God told them that he was going to give them another one to take Saul's place. God called the prophet Samuel and told him to go to the house of a man named Jesse. God was going to make one of Jesse's sons king. So Samuel went. *(Walk five or six steps and knock on a pretend door.)*

When Jesse came to the door, Samuel said, "Bring your sons here. God is going to make one of them king." So Jesse brought his sons in and lined them up in front of Samuel — 1-2-3-4-5-6-7 — according to their size. *(With your hand, show a stairway — start at 6'4", perhaps, and go down.)*

Samuel looked at the biggest one and thought, "Ah, this is he. He's big and strong. He will make a good king." But God said, "*No!* Not that one!" So Samuel went to the next biggest. Again, God said *no*. And so to the next, then the next, and the next, and finally to the last one. But God still said *no* — not one of these. By this time, Samuel was getting worried. "Do you have any more sons, Jesse?"

"Sure," Jesse said. "There is one more, but he is just a little squirt. He's out watching the sheep."

"Bring him in," Samuel said. When Jesse did, God said, "He's the one." And the *smallest* son became King *David!*

* **I Samuel 16:7-13**

So never worry how big or little you are. Just tell God you want to be what he wants you to be, and he will have a wonderful life for you.

#16

DID ADAM PLANT THAT TREE?*

God's Word

(Take a large apple from your pocket. While the children watch, polish it carefully; hold it up to admire. Polish it a little more. Hold it up again. Then, take a big bite — chew it up slowly, savoring it. Then wipe your mouth. Don't rush this part. The more time you take, the greater the interest you will create. Then say:)
Boy, this is a good-tasting apple, isn't it? Apples are good, aren't they? Aren't you enjoying this one? You're not? Boy, I sure am! Now, I don't know where this one was grown, but I wish it were in my back yard. Now, where do you suppose the very first apple tree was? *(Wait for an answer.)* In the Garden of Eden? Maybe. But we don't know for sure. But don't you suppose that this apple came from a tree, that came from a tree, that came from a tree, that came from a tree, that came from a tree *(say this part with increasing rapidity)*, that came from the very first apple tree that God put on this earth? I think so.
Let's cut this apple in half. Do you see these seeds? Why did God put them there? Right! So we could plant more apple trees. How many seeds would it take to start a tree? That's right — just one of these small seeds would grow up to be a big tree.
Isn't it wonderful how God planned it? How many apples do you suppose you could get from that tree? Yes, maybe a hundred, maybe two hundred — and every year for as long as the tree lives.
Now let's talk about a different kind of planting that God does. The seed is very different, and God does not plant it in soil. It's not planted in our garden. Can you think of what that seed is? Well, if we let him, if we will accept it, God

* Luke 8:11

plants his *word* in our hearts. And if we water and feed it every day by reading the Bible and praying, it will *grow*. Then we can go out and plant that same word in somebody else's heart. An apple tree with hundreds of apples can grow from one of these tiny seeds. *(Hold up an apple half.)* So, if God's word is planted in your heart, and you plant it in somebody else's heart by telling them about Jesus, and they do the same thing, why, five hundred years from now, if the world lasts that long, somebody can know Jesus and go to heaven because of the seed *you* planted.

(You might want to give each child an apple and say:) This is so that you kids will think about planting God's word.

#17

WHY DID I GET LEFT OUT?*

God's Calling

(This story was told by our son, a pastor. Obviously, the people and facts will have to be changed to conform to what is true of the storyteller — ideally, the pastor. It's given here just as it was originally told so that you can see the possibilities.)

When I was the age of some of you, I lived in Highland Park, California. One of the kids I played with every day was a boy named Lloyd. You know, it seemed as though Lloyd could do anything he wanted to. He could stay up as late as he wanted to every night, and I don't think he ever had to do any homework. I remember on Halloween nights, he could stay out trick-or-treating until eleven o'clock! I sure wished then I could do what Lloyd could do. I just couldn't see why I couldn't.

When I got to high school, my sister was one of the most popular girls in school. She was a cheerleader, campus queen and everything. I sure wished I could be that popular. Another of my sisters had a boyfriend named Charlie. He was the school's six-foot-two, two-hundred-and-thirty-pound star fullback. Charlie could knock down the other team's linemen like bowling pins. I wasn't very big then, and I might have had trouble knocking down some of you. Why

* **Psalm 139:13-16**

couldn't *I* be a big fullback? There were lots of other people I wished I could be like.

Have you ever wished you could be like somebody else? I'm sure I wondered lots of times why God didn't let me do and be all the things my friends could do and be.

Now, if I had been listening, God would have told me, "Now, Dan, I don't want you to be like those other people. I've got something else in mind just for you — something I want *you* to be." And do you know what? *Now* I know *just* what it is. I am and I'm doing what I *most* want to *do* and *be* — a *preacher* in *this* church, right here, right now.

Don't ever envy anyone. Just ask God to show you what he wants you to be, and, you will see, he has something special, just for you.

#18

I WANT PEOPLE TO LIKE ME*

Being Close to Jesus

(Obtain a spoked wheel, the larger, the better; or draw a large picture of a spoked wheel.)
What have we got here this morning? A spoked wheel, isn't it? These are the spokes. Wheels are wonderful things, aren't they? Boy, your bike and your dad's car surely wouldn't be much good without wheels, would they?

You know, I was thinking: all of us want people to like us, don't we? You all want to be popular with the kids at school and in your neighborhood. You want the other kids to want you to come over and play with them, don't you? It's no fun always being by ourselves. And God wants us to have friends, to have fun, to have people like us.

Were you wondering what this wheel is for? This wheel has a secret for you. This wheel is going to show you how you can be the kind of kid that people will really like. Now, the Bible tells us that God wants Jesus to be the center of our life. *(Point to the hub.)* Let's pretend that Jesus is in the center and each of these spokes is one of us. I'm sure that we would all agree that the closer we get to Jesus, the nicer

* **James 4:8**

kids we will be, because Jesus makes us that way. Now look —
here is something special I've learned. *(Run your fingers
down the spokes toward the hub.)* The closer we get to Jesus,
the closer we get to these other people *(point to the other
spokes near the hub)*, and the more they will like us, and
the more we will like them. Look — we are having a wonderful time, because we're gathered around Jesus. So you see,
the secret to having people like you is to stay close to Jesus.

#19

LINKS IN THE CHAIN*

Holding on to God

(Provide a piece of chain with fairly large links.)
Well, kids, what am I holding? Right — it's a chain.
(Pull on it.) It's a real strong one, lots stronger than rope.
It's made of steel. You know, some chains are so strong, they
could lift this whole room without breaking.

Did you notice that this chain is made up of a lot of
links, all sort of holding fingers? *(Show what you mean by
locking together the thumb and forefinger of each of your
hands.)* Do chains ever break? Oh, yes, and sometimes when
they do, things get damaged. People even get killed. Now
let's pretend we were lifting that piano *(or some other large
object)*, using this chain, and it broke. *Crash!* Now, would
all the links break? No, just one. Which one? Right! The
weakest one. Does it matter how strong the ones are that
didn't break? No! No chain is any stronger than the weakest
link.

Now I'm going to tell you something I'm sure you have
never thought about. You may not even believe me, but it's
true. *(Point to a chain link with each example which follows.)*
Do you know that each one of you is making a chain? I don't
mean one made out of colored paper to hang on a Christmas
tree, but you are making a chain, link by link. One of the
links is your mind. Everything you read in school, or study,
or hear your teacher or your mom and dad tell you, is making
one link. If you pay attention and study hard, it will be a
strong link. *(Point.)* You need this, and all your life, you are

* Galatians 6:7-9

going to be glad you built a good one.

Another link is your body, your health. You're building this by how you eat — you know, by not eating a lot of sweet, junky food — by getting a lot of good exercise, getting enough sleep, taking care of the wonderful body the Lord gave you. Oh, this link needs to be real strong, and you're building it every day.

There are a lot of other links, too, but do you know the most important one? *(Pause.)* It's the one you are building by coming to church and Sunday school today. The most important link in your life's chain is the one that links you to Jesus. Every time you pray, every time you read the Bible, listen to your pastor or Sunday school teacher, you're making that link stronger. It will help you hold onto God, no matter what. In the end, it doesn't matter how strong your mind link is, or how strong your body link is. These links can't save you — only the one that links you to Jesus can save you.

#20

A REAL CHRISTMAS PRESENT*

Unselfish Giving

I've got a question for you: What is a gift? *(Pause.)* Well, really, a gift is something you give to someone because you want him or her to have it, and you don't expect him or her to give you anything back.

Now, if you say, "I'm going to give Suzy a five-dollar doll for Christmas, and she had better spend five dollars on the present she gives me.", would that be a gift? No, you would only be exchanging Christmas presents with Suzy, wouldn't you? Let me tell you a story, and you will see what I mean.

Now let's pretend I'm walking down *(local street name)* _____ . It's real cold, and I'm wearing my very warm ski jacket with my parka hood covering my ears. The cold wind is whistling, but I'm warm and comfortable. As I'm walking, I see a man on the other side of the street. Oh, he looks so cold and so poor. His thin, soiled

* **Luke 14:12-14**

jacket is even torn, and his ears are almost blue
So I walk across the street, take off my nice wai
and say, "Here, friend, I don't want you to be cold
Take my jacket."

Now, was that a real gift? It was, wasn't it? He couldn't pay me back. He couldn't give me anything in return — only his own torn, dirty jacket. Did you know that's what Jesus does for us? When we become Christians, when we ask Jesus to be our Savior, he gives us what the Bible calls his robe of righteousness — a sort of jacket of his goodness. This covers up all our sins, and we don't need to have cold hearts again, ever.

That last part was not pretend. Why don't we, each of us, try to give at least one real gift this Christmas, shall we? I know Jesus will be pleased . . . because he made Christmas.

#21

DON'T TAKE A DETOUR*

God's Route to Heaven

(Place a road map and a Bible in a large paper grocery bag. Do not flatten the bag.)

I've got something in here, and I'm sure you'll never guess what it is. Anyone want to try? It's about this big *(show 18" x 18")*; it's just covered with lines; and some people would never go anywhere without one. Other people don't think they need one, and sometimes, they get lost. Can anybody guess? With it, you could find your way to every McDonald's in *(your state)* _____ .
(Take out the map and unfold it.) A road map.

You know, actually, I have two road maps. The second one is even better than the first. In fact, it's the best map that ever was. If you'll pay attention to it, it will tell you when to stop and when to go. It will tell you how to avoid some of the deserts, show you where the dangerous curves are and where the hidden bumps are. It show you how to stay away from places that have pretty names and look as

* Isaiah 30:19-21

though they would be so much fun, but are very bad for us. It will take you to places that are really fun, the kind of fun God wants us to have. And do you know, it shows you a road, plainly marked on the map, that will take you to the most wonderful place that could ever be. You know who you'll see when you get there? Jesus! We think he will be at the door to welcome us into heaven.

So now, what's the map I have in this bag? The Bible, of course — God's road map. *(Take the Bible from the bag and open it.)* Now let's look to see if this is true. *(Read Isaiah 30:19-21.)* Satan would try to get us on the road with dangerous curves and places that would wreck us, but God's road map *(hold up the Bible)* shows up just where those places are, and gives us a better road to follow.

Now, God's road leads through some dry deserts, some roads that are real bumpy, and we might think, "Boy, why did God let me come down this way?" But God knows we need this to make us strong. We can't see him, but he's on that road with us. He promised. And if Jesus is our Savior and Lord, he will lead us right up to the gate of heaven. But let me warn you: don't take any detours! The devil is always alongside the road, whispering, "Hey, look, this is a better road." Don't believe it. Remember, God says he's a *liar*.

#22

CREATURE OF DARKNESS*

God's Light

Good morning, kids.

I was wondering if you have any big rocks in your yard, or maybe some large plants in pots that are resting on the bare ground. If you do, you have got some creatures living under them that you almost never see. If you do have anything like this in your yard, try an experiment. When you get home, just pick up a rock or a pot and look underneath. You might have to look quickly, of course, because the bugs that you will see will run quickly to find some other dark place to hide. They hate the light, because they are

* I John 1:7

creatures of darkness. They love to be in the dark, because
nobody can see them there. Nobody can see what they are
doing. Now this is all right for them, because God made
them creatures of darkness. Did you know that God talks
about this in the Bible? He says he doesn't want us to walk
in darkness, but to walk in the light. But God is not really
talking about daytime and nighttime.

Let me explain. Did you ever do anything that you
knew you shouldn't have, and you were afraid your mom or
dad, or maybe your teacher, would find out? So you avoided
them and hid? That's what the Bible means by walking in
darkness. Suppose I had an argument with *(name of a person
known to kids)* _____ and was
mad at him *(or her)*. So whenever I saw him *(or her)*, I'd look
the other way, or walk on the other side of the room so I
wouldn't meet him *(or her)*. God says that's walking in darkness. But God wants us to walk in the light — with him,
and with everybody else.

Now, how do we do this? Well, as soon as I realize I've
done something I shouldn't have done, I must ask God to forgive me. And then if I've hurt somebody, or if I've done something that I ought to confess to my mom and dad, I do it right
away. And do you know what? The moment I do, I step out
of the darkness and into the light — and I feel so good after
I've done it. I feel good with God, with mom and dad, and
with anyone else to whom I've apologized.

Now, just so you will know that this is really what
God says, listen to what he wrote in his book, the Bible. "If
we walk in the light as Jesus is in the light, then we have
fellowship with each other, and the blood of Jesus Christ,
God's Son, cleanses us from all sin."

And whenever you are tempted to do anything that
you would have to hide, just think of those creeping things
that hide under the rocks in your garden.

#23

DO I HAVE TO DO IT

NOW, LORD?*

Obedience

Good morning, kids.

I've got a riddle for you. Do you like riddles? Easy ones or hard ones? The easy ones aren't as much fun, though, so I'm going to ask you a hard one. Now, you really know the answer, if you will just think. You mom and dad know it — this I know for sure. OK, here it is. Listen very carefully. Of all the things boys and girls make, what do they make most often? *(Wait for answers. Express pleasure over each one.)* Any more? Fine! Those were all good, but you still haven't got the right one.

The thing that boys and girls make most often is . . . *excuses.* That's right . . . *excuses.* I'm going to give you a list of excuses, and you see if you made any of these this week. OK? Now, listen *(let your face and your voice express the emotion that would naturally accompany each excuse as you say it):*

> "I didn't have time."
> "It wasn't my turn."
> "I was too tired."
> "I didn't hear you."
> "He hit me first."
> "Can't I do it later?"
> "I don't like that job."

Now, did you make any of those this week? *(If you get no answer, say: "Are you sure?" . . . or . . . "I thought so." — whatever is appropriate.)*

Now, do you know who made the very first excuse that was ever made? *(Wait for an answer.)* Adam did. . . . Do you remember what it was? God asked him if he had eaten the fruit off the tree that he had been told not to touch, and he made the very first excuse. He said that it was his wife's fault; she gave the fruit to him.

* **I Peter 5:2-4**

Can you think of any others in the Bible who made excuses? Well, Moses did. When God told him to go back to Egypt and tell Pharaoh to let his people go, Moses said *(with complaining voice)*, "I can't, Lord, I don't talk very well; send my brother!"

Now, suppose when Jesus called his disciples to come and work for him, they said, "Aw, do I have to come now, Jesus? I just started to play with my slot cars."; or, "Can't you wait until this TV show is over?"; or, "Do I have to do it now? I'm tired!"; or, "Can't somebody else do it? It's too hard!"

Do you know what would have happened? I think we would have had some different apostles, and nobody would have ever heard about Peter, James and John again.

So when God calls us to do something, we had better do just what the disciples did — drop everything and come running.

And when your mom and dad call you, do the same thing. You'll be happier, your mom and dad will be happier, and most of all, God will be able to do something special with you, just as he did with the disciples.

#24

LOOK AT THAT CRAZY NOAH!*

Following God Isn't Always Easy

Do you kids like boats? Did you ever try to build one or sail on one? If you were going to build a big boat and go sailing on the ocean, what would you need? *(Pause.)* Wood, motor, propeller . . . yes, you would need all those and a lot more, besides. And then, when you got all those things together, what's the next thing you would do? *(Pause.)* That's right — put them all together and make your boat. Now, before you could sail in it, you would need one more thing. What is that? *Water.* Sure, ships sail on water.

Now suppose you built that boat miles and miles from any water, and you had no way to get your boat to the ocean. What would people think? What would they say? Boy, they

* **Genesis 6:12-22**

sure would laugh at you, wouldn't they? Ha, ha, ha! *(Practice a hearty laugh. You're going to need it for this story.)* "Look what somebody's doing — building a big boat, and there's no water for it to sail on!" Can't you just hear them laughing?

But do you know, that's probably what they did to Noah when he built the ark? He built it miles and miles from any water. It was a huge boat. There was no way Noah could get that boat to the ocean. *(Laugh uproariously.)* "Look at that crazy Noah, building that boat! *(Laugh again.)* What does he think he is doing?" But every day, Noah kept on building the ark, building it just the way God told him to. The people laughed, but Noah kept right on building, day after day, year after year. It probably wasn't much fun to hear all those bad people laugh and make fun of him. And these were very bad people — not just because they laughed, but they were so bad in so many ways that God said he was going to wipe them off the face of the earth. That's why Noah was building the ark — to save his family and the animals.

Of course, when the animals came into the ark, the people probably laughed all the more: "Look what old Noah is doing *now* — putting a zoo on his boat!" *(At this point, the storyteller should react to an imagined raindrop that has fallen on his head, then put out his hand as though feeling for more drops.)* It started to rain. Well, that maybe didn't bother the people watching. They just laughed at the rain. But when the water started to climb up to their ankles, then to their knees, the laughing was *all over,* and they were scared.

Inside the ark, do you suppose Noah was laughing? having the last laugh? No, I don't think so. He knew these people were very wicked, but Noah was a good man, and it made him sad to see all those people drown. But that was the only way God could clean up the earth.

This story shows us that even way back then, people laughed at other people who followed God. Kids may even laugh at you if you try to live the way God wants you to. Just pray for them. They don't know what they are doing.

#25

DON'T DROP YOUR BABY*

Learning Hard Lessons

Have you kids ever seen an eagle flying? Eagles are beautiful birds, aren't they? They can fly *so* high, until they're just a speck in the sky. Do you know they ride on the wind? They spread their wings, the wind lifts them, and they can sail for hours, way, way up in the sky. How do you suppose they learn to fly that way? Does God teach them, or does the mother eagle?

Well, one thing we know, when the mother of the eaglets — that's what baby eagles are called — thinks it's time for her eaglets to fly, she picks one up in her long claws and flies high in the sky; higher and higher she flies with her baby. Then she *drops* him. . . . Down and down the eaglet falls, tumbling over and over. *(Use lots of gestures here. Pointing over your head, show the eaglet tumbling.)* Then the mother swoops down and catches her baby, just in time. And she goes up again, just as high. Do you think she will be more careful this time? No, she does it *again*. Down again, that eaglet falls. This time, he flaps his wings a little, but still, he's falling. Again, down swoops the mother and catches her baby, just in time. Do you suppose that eaglet is beginning to think his mommy doesn't love him very much, especially when she drops him a *third* time? Now, this time, that eaglet really flaps his wings the way he should, and do you know what? *He can fly!* He can, *really*! Now he knows his mother loves him, after all. She just had to do this so that he, too, could fly high, fast and far.

Did you ever think that maybe your mommy didn't love you when she made you do something you didn't want to do, or something that was very hard? or when you couldn't do something you really wanted to do or go somewhere you badly wanted to go?

Or maybe you even think sometimes that God doesn't love you when bad or scary things happen. If you ever think like that, just remember the eagle story. God told that eagle what to do so that her baby would fly. And you can't always understand why your mom and dad ask you to do things you

* **Proverbs 30:18-19**

might not want to, or don't let you do some things you want to do very much. It's for the same reason: so you can grow up to be just what God wants you to be, and do all the wonderful things he has planned for you.

#26
THE LORD IS MY STRENGTH*
Giving Burdens to God

Have you kids ever watched a weight-lifter? You know, how they put big wheels on the ends of a bar and lift it over their heads? *(Demonstrate.)* It would be nice to have muscles like that. Think of all the heavy things you could pick up. It would be so much easier to carry out the trash for your mom or clean up your room. Doesn't that sound exciting? Well, you could use your muscles for fun things, too.

(Have a box or a briefcase that looks as though one of the smaller nearby children could lift it. Ask one of them to bring it to you. You will have filled it with heavy books or anything too heavy for the child to lift. When he tries to do so and fails, say:) That's too heavy for you, isn't it? Let me help. *(Both of you lift and carry the object.)* You see, it was too heavy for *(name of child)* ⎯⎯⎯⎯⎯⎯⎯⎯⎯ , but when I added my strength, it was easy. That's what God does for us. There are lots of things that are hard for us, aren't there — things we really need help with, and it seems nobody can or will help. That's when we should talk to Jesus about it. Say: "Jesus, I need your help. This is too hard for me."

Now, nothing is too hard or too heavy for God. There is a Bible verse that tells us this. *(Name of child)* ⎯⎯⎯⎯ ⎯⎯⎯⎯⎯⎯⎯ and I will show you. *(Show him, probably best beforehand, how to hold his right arm at a right angle, making a muscle.)* Now, *(child's name)* ⎯⎯⎯⎯⎯⎯⎯ ⎯⎯⎯⎯⎯ , tell the rest of the kids what the Bible says. *(Arrange ahead of time for him to say: "God is my muscles.")* Is that really what the Bible says? Let's read it. *(Read Psalm 27:1.)* It does say that, doesn't it? God will be strong for us, if we ask him.

* Psalm 27:1

#27

HUMAN BUILDING BLOCKS*

The Family of God

This is a nice church we have, isn't it? Do you know how it was made? What did they do first? They started at the bottom with the foundation. What came next? Walls? Yes, and then what? A roof to keep out the rain. What materials did they use? Cement, wood, plaster, nails.

Now, I wonder, did you know there is a house that's built of people? Yes, there is — not cement, not wood, but people. And it's a beautiful house, the most beautiful house that was ever built. Actually, it's not finished yet, but every day, new people get put into place, just like building blocks. *(Show blocks being set in place.)* And this may surprise you: these people are *alive* when they are set into the wall. You all look as though you didn't believe me. Now, what can I do that will show you that what I'm saying is true? I know, I'll prove it from the Bible. You'll believe that, won't you? Now listen, I'll read it to you. *(Read I Peter 2:4-5.)*

So you see, God is building a temple; and if we are Christians, we are blocks in that temple. Every time another person gives his heart to Jesus, he becomes another building block. This building *(point to church wall)* is made of wood and plaster, but God is building his house, his temple, with us. And you know that if a building is going to be strong, it has to have strong lumber and all the blocks have to fit together closely. That's why *we* have to be strong Christians, and get along with each other. We want to fit together, don't we? We can't fight or argue or say mean things about each other. That surely wouldn't build a good wall, would it? But if we love each other and love Jesus, he can build a strong, beautiful house, using you and me. Isn't that something special?

---

* I Peter 2:4-5

#28

OPEN UP; IT'S ME!*

Jesus Waits

"Here I am, I stand at the door and knock. If anyone hears my voice and opens the door, I will go in."

I wonder why Jesus doesn't just come in. All he had to do was turn the knob or push the little lever down — all doors have them. Did you ever see a door without something to open it on the outside?

Suppose one day I came to your house. I rang your doorbell or knocked, and you were helping your mom mix some dough, or maybe make some meatloaf, and both of you had your hands in the bowl, all covered with food. *(Demonstrate.)* So you yelled, "Who is it?"

I said, "It's *(storyteller's name)* _____ ."

"Oh," your mom said, "come on in." Well, I'd open the door and come in.

But suppose there wasn't any doorknob on the door. Then what would I do? Knock again, this time even louder? Suppose I did, and again your mom said, "Come in!" But because there was no knob, what would I do? I'd stay outside until somebody opened the door from the inside of the house, wouldn't I?

So you see, that's what Jesus meant. Let's read that verse again: "Here I am, I stand at the door and knock. If anyone hears my voice and opens the door, I will go in." He's talking about the door to your heart, that can be opened only from the inside. You have to open it. Jesus would never push it open. If you want Jesus to be your Lord and Savior, you have to tell him so and invite him in. If you want him to be king of your life, to show you what to do, to tell you how to act, he will — if you ask him, if you open the door. Remember, you are the only one who has the key to the door of your heart.

* **Revelations 3:20**

#29

WHEN DID WE DO THAT FOR YOU, JESUS?*

Sharing God's Love

Let's do a little pretending this morning, shall we? Only it's not really pretend, because this really happened.

Now, once upon a time, long, long ago, there were some people who lived over there, on that side of the street. *(Point to one side of the church, but not to suggest any part of the congregation.)* Every day, people passed by who were sick, but nobody cared or tried to help them. Some people came by who were very hungry, and even though it was dinner time and there was plenty of food, no one asked them to come in and eat. People came by who were so hot and tired, and they couldn't even get a drink of water. And though the people living on that side of the street had lots of clothes, even some they didn't need at all, they wouldn't give anything to those people who came by who were practically naked.

But the people on the *other* side of the street *(point)* were not like that at all. Whenever somebody came who was hungry, they would feed him. If he was sick, they took care of him. They gave him clothes and were friendly with him.

One day, King Jesus came to those people. He said to the kind, generous ones on that side of the street *(point to second side)*, "Oh, you are really blessed people. When I was hungry, you fed me. When I was sick, you took care of me. When I didn't have enough to wear, you gave me clothes."

Those people were *so surprised*! They said, "Lord, we don't remember ever doing any of those things for you."

"But you did," Jesus said. "When you did it for my poor, sick, hungry brothers and sisters, you did it for *me.*"

But listen to what he said to those people on the *other* side, the ones who were selfish and unkind. *(Read Matthew*

* **Matthew 25:31-46**

25:41-46.) Boy, we sure would not want that to happen to us, would we?

Now, doesn't that make you want to help people who are poor, who are hungry and sick and need a friend? Why, think of it: we are doing it for Jesus!

#30
CANDLES FOR THE KING*
Giving Your Best

Do you kids like fantasy stories? You know, stories about kings and princes and dragons and brave knights? Now listen carefully. This happened thousands of years ago in Never-neverland. A king was going to take his army out of his castle at midnight to fight a battle with a wicked king in the next city. He wanted to surprise the wicked king.

The king knew it would be pitch black, so he asked all his people to burn a candle during the night so the soldiers wouldn't walk off the road. Everybody got real excited. Some of them bought very fancy candles that cost lots of dollars, or they spent many days decorating their candles to light the way. Some candles were in beautiful colors and shapes. The people said, "The king will surely notice these." The night finally came, and *it was dark* — no moon, no stars.

Some people stood along the road in front of their houses. The ones with the fanciest, most expensive candles just put them in their windows. But down by the river, there was a narrow bridge that the king and his soldiers had to cross to get to the other city. A young boy stood there with his candle. There was nothing at all special about his candle. It was just a plain, ordinary one, but he held it high, because he surely didn't want any soldier to miss the bridge and fall in the river. All night long he held it, in case some soldiers might be late crossing, or some might be injured in the battle and come back early.

But the king won a big victory, and he and his troops started back home. It was just getting light when they got to the bridge again. The king came first, and he noticed that

* **I Corinthians 4:2**

the little boy's candle had burned down almost to his fingers. The wax had even run down and burned them a little.

The next day, the king called everybody to the palace. He said, "Come and bring your candle. I have a prize for one of you." They all lined up before him, holding their candles. The ones with the real fancy, expensive ones said, "I know I'm going to win." The king noticed, though, that the very fancy ones weren't burned much. He knew they were only lit for a little while. He walked right past *them.* Down to the end of the line he went, to the little boy. "*This* is the one. You let your light shine where we needed it most. You stayed all night in the cold." The king put his big arm around the boy and said, "*You win the prize.*" You are number one in my kingdom."

You see, the king wanted to see lights, not fancy candles, and that's what God wants from us. He said we are to let our light shine in dark places so that people can find Jesus. He doesn't care about our color, or how fancy we are dressed, or what we look like. He only wants to see our light.

If you love Jesus and do what he wants and go where he wants you to go, your light will shine.

#31

GOD'S PHONE NUMBER*

Prayer

(You'll need a telephone; or you can pretend that you are holding one.)

Good morning, kids! *(Hold the telephone. Dial or push numbers for a few moments.)*

Telephones are marvelous things, aren't they? Think of all the wonderful things you can do with a telephone. Now, for instance, I could call up the *(name of local establishment)* _____ : "Hello, is this the *(name)* _____ ? Will you rush over *(number)* _____ special deluxe strawberry-marshmallow-pineapple sundaes to *(name of your church)* _____ right away?" . . . Maybe

* Jeremiah 33:3

I'd better not do that. It would be kind of messy. But just think. . . . I can dial this phone and talk to somebody halfway around the world.

Of course, sometimes telephones make you mad. Maybe you are outside your house and you run in to answer the phone *(pick up the receiver)*: "Hello? . . . *No*! This is *not* Louie's Pizza Parlor!" *(Hang up.)* Or there is somebody you really have to talk to, and you call and call all day, but no answer. Or every time you call, you get a busy signal — bzzz, bzzz, bzzz.

Do you know what somebody told me? That God has a telephone number, just the way we have. Can you believe that? Can any of you guess what it is? Well, I'll tell you. Now listen closely so you will remember: it's JERE-333. Did you get that? JERE-333. I think some of you still don't believe me, so I will show you. Let's look in God's phone book, Jeremiah 33:3: "Call on me and I will answer you and tell you great and unsearchable things you do not know." So you see, you can call God any time. Now if somebody called me at three in the morning, I wouldn't be mad, but I wouldn't be much fun to talk to. I'd be so sleepy. But the Bible says that God never sleeps, and his ear is always open to hear us.

Now if I were to call *(any foreign country)* _____ _____ , it would cost lots of dollars, but we can talk to God in *heaven,* and it doesn't cost a *penny.* And we will never get a busy signal, even though ten thousand other people are talking to him at the *same* time. You can talk as long as you want, the longer, the better. You can tell him when you're happy, when you are sad, when you feel bad because you did something you shouldn't have, when you don't know what to do, when you've just got to have help. . . . You don't need any buttons, any dials, any wires. No matter where you are, just close your eyes and say, "Dear Lord Jesus, I need to talk to you," and God will be listening. He promised.

#32

FIVE LOAVES, TWO FISHES*

Miracles in Giving

Do you remember about that time in the Bible when Jesus wanted to feed five thousand people? He asked the disciples if they had any food. "No, we don't," they said, "but there's a boy here who has five little loaves and two fishes, but that's his lunch. It sure wouldn't feed this crowd."

Jesus said, "It's enough. Tell all the people to sit down." Then, you remember, Jesus took that boy's lunch and blessed it, and multiplied it so that everybody had enough. There was even some left over. In fact, there was more left over than the little boy gave Jesus in the first place. Wasn't that a miracle?!

But suppose that little boy had been selfish. Suppose he'd said, "*No!* This is my lunch. Let them get their own. I'm not giving up my lunch for anybody!" Would all those people have gone hungry? *(Pause for answer.)* Well, I don't think so. I think Jesus would have fed them some other way. But if that little boy had said *no,* just think what he would have missed — a chance to help Jesus in his work. Why, two thousand years later, we are still reading about what Jesus and that little boy did. That's why we should always share what we have, always try to bring an offering to Sunday school, no matter how small. Whatever we give or do for Jesus, he can multiply a hundred times.

#33

X-RAYS**

A Pure Heart and Mouth

You know, kids, we've had a lot of wonderful inventions, haven't we? Can any of you name a few? *(Pause for answers.)* Yes, all of those are very valuable, aren't they? The one I'm thinking of is the X-ray. Do you all know what

* **John 6:9-14**
** **Proverbs 4:23-24**

an X-ray machine is? Well, it takes a picture of the inside of your body. If you swallowed a small toy, or even a pin, a doctor could tell just where that was in your stomach. The X-ray picture would show him.

Maybe you won't believe it, but I invented another kind of X-ray. Well, I didn't really invent it, I just discovered it. You know, the Bible talks a lot about the heart. Give your heart to Jesus. And don't let your heart be afraid, and things like that.

Now, God is not talking about the heart in our body that pumps the blood through our arteries. No, he's talking about what we really are, what makes us do what we do, say what we say, think what we think. I can't tell what you kids are like by looking at your faces, but I've got an X-ray on my body that tells me if you're mean or kind; if you're jealous or happy because other people have good things; or if you think you are better than other people. It tells me if you love Jesus.

Now, I can see you don't believe me. You think I'm kidding. Of course, the best way to prove anything is to prove it from the Bible, and the Bible says that your mouth is going to say what your heart is filled with. So you see, I just have to point my ear — my X-ray machine — toward you *(do so)*, and from what you say, what you talk about, I can tell just what you are. Your words paint a picture of what your heart and your mind are like. Now, of course, you can do the same with me. You also have an X-ray ear; we all do.

Boy, that means we really have to watch how we talk, don't we? Yes, but when we know we are saying things we shouldn't, when we realize our words aren't kind, what should we do? Clamp our mouths shut? No, what we really need to do is to say, "Lord, forgive me for thinking bad thoughts that make me say bad things. Take away all my meanness, and make me more like Jesus."

Then you can talk all you want.

SECTION III

SIN

#34

WHAT'S BROKEN CAN BE FIXED*

Forgiveness

Did you kids ever break one of your mom's dishes or vases? I know I sure did when I was a kid. Sometimes, things just slip out of your hands, and then, *crash!*

Of course, if it's just something cheap, your mom might not get too mad, but some things are very valuable, maybe unique, one of a kind. That means there was no other made that was just like that. If you break something like that, it's gone forever.

Maybe your mom and dad would try to put it back together if they could. They'd hunt all over the floor to be sure they got all the pieces. Then they'd get a tube of cementing glue, and piece by piece, they would glue the vase back together. Sometimes this works, but often, you can see it's just patched up. The cracks and chips still show, and it doesn't really look beautiful anymore. Your mom's one-of-a-kind vase is just ready for the trash can.

Did you know God made each of you one of a kind? He did. That's why you're so special. There is nobody else like you. You're more precious to Jesus than any very valuable vase, no matter how much it costs. Can you think how God's special people like you can get broken? *(Pause. Respond to answers, but the one you want is "when we sin.")* That's right. When we sin, we kind of spoil what God made. We are not just the way God wants us to be.

Does he look at us and say, "Too bad — not good for anything now but the trash can."? Oh, no — he loves us, he made us; we are too valuable to him, even though we have sinned. And if we bring the broken pieces to him — you know, tell him we are sorry that we did something that we shouldn't have — and we ask him to forgive us, he does forgive us. He mends our hearts. And you know what else? He makes them just as good as new — no cracks, no chips. It's just as if we had never sinned.

* Colossians 2:13-14

#35

YOU SHOULD HAVE GIVEN THAT TO ME*

Envy

(Obtain a pair of eyeglasses which are no longer used. Glue to the lenses two cardboard cylinders from rolls of toilet tissue. Secure them so that when you put on the glasses, you look through the tubes. Put the glasses in a box.)

Good morning, kids. I've got something really interesting in this box, and I'm sure you could never guess what it is. Anybody want to try? OK, let's look. *(Remove the glasses from the box and put them on.)* Did you ever see anybody who looks like this? No? Really? These are called see-what-somebody-else-has glasses. Lots of people wear them. I think you do, sometimes. When I wear glasses like this, I can't see any of the good things God has given me. All I can see is what he has given somebody else — things I wish I had. This is called envy — so these are envy glasses. When you envy somebody for something he has, do you know what you are saying? "God, you made a mistake — you should have given those things to *me* instead." Now, God never makes a mistake, and if we will just take off our envy glasses *(remove them)*, we can see all the good things he has given us.

Now, for instance, I won't be happy with my Sears bike *(put on the glasses again)* if I'm looking at your classy ten-speed Schwinn racing bike, wishing it were mine. *(Remove the glasses.)* And you girls won't enjoy the new dress your mom bought you if you are always looking *(put on the glasses again)* at what someone else is wearing that costs more.

Whenever you find yourself envying, just rip off those see-what-somebody-else-has glasses. *(Rip the cylinders off the glasses, and then put on the glasses again.)* Then you really will be able to see how good God is to you.

And you really can begin to enjoy everything you have.

* **Luke 12:15**

(handwritten annotations:)

bad attitude

things that don't go the way I want them to.

The problem with B-A glasses is that it always reminds your day, family rating time with friends church

#36

BUT I ONLY TOOK ONE*

Free Will

(You'll need one large cookie jar with a lid, and one cookie for each child and for you.)
Good morning, kids. Do you see my nice cookie jar? Do you know what's in it? But before we talk about that, I want to ask you a question. Did you ever wish that God had made you so . . . it . . . *(Say each word separately. As you do, walk as a robot would for a few steps.)* was . . . not . . . pos- . . . si- . . . ble . . . for . . . you . . . to . . . do . . . any- . . . thing . . . bad? . . . That . . . it . . . was . . . not . . . pos- . . . si- . . . ble . . . to . . . sin? . . . So . . . we . . . had . . . to . . . do . . . every- . . . thing . . . just . . . as . . . he . . . said?

That wouldn't be much fun, would it? No, God made us each different, and he gave us a *free* will. That means we don't *have* to do what God wants us to, but we will, of course, be sorry if we don't. God wants us to do what is right, and he gives us parents, Sunday school teachers and pastors to help us. And he has given us his word, the Bible. One of the things the Bible says is that we should not give in to temptation. What does this mean? . . . That's right. Don't do anything God says is wrong, even though you want to very much.

Let me show you what I mean. Let's take this cookie jar. What do you suppose it's full of ? Right, yummy cookies. Do you think they're yummy? I *know* they are! *(Rub your stomach.)* Now, I'm going to put this jar right here and pretend that I am one of you.

Let's pretend that your mom has said, "Don't you take a cookie before dinner. I'm going shopping and I will be back in an hour." So you go out and play for ten minutes, and come in *so* hungry — and there is that cookie jar. Ohhhhh! You want one *so* much. So you just lift the lid a little bit and look in. Now, you shouldn't have done that, because now you want one *even more.* You go get a drink of milk, and all you can think of is how good one of those cookies would taste with milk. So you come back and you take off the lid *(do so)*, and put your hand in just to see how heavy the cookies are.

* **I Corinthians 10:13**

You put the cookie back. But you don't walk away. You just stand there with your hand right above the jar. Then, finally *(take a quick look around first)*, you reach in and take a cookie and eat it. *(Eat one.)* You shouldn't have done that. *(Look sad.)* In a few minutes, your cookie is gone, and you're worried your mom is going to ask you if you took one, and you know God didn't like it!

You see, you did just what God said we must *not* do — give in to temptation. What was the first thing I did that was wrong? It was when I lifted the jar, wasn't it? The second thing was to *lift it again*. The third mistake was to stand there with my hand over the jar. By that time, it was *too late*. So what do you do when you are tempted? Walk away. Close your eyes or your ears. Ask Jesus to help you. He will!

#37
OUT OF THE SAME MOUTH*
Praises and Curses

Do you kids like to hike in the mountains? I think it's so special. The air is so clear; the water is so good to drink whenever you can find a spring. I'm going to tell you a story, and when I'm done, I want you to tell me if it really happened.

One vacation time, I was climbing to the top of Mount *(name a mountain kids would know)* _____ . We had been hiking for three or four hours, and I was so hot and thirsty and tired. Boy, I really needed a drink. Then suddenly, just ahead of us, we saw a little spring of water shooting out of the rocks. Oh, what water . . . so cool, so clear . . . it sparkled like diamonds. I dropped down on my knees and drank and drank . . . but suddenly, it turned bitter, and got yellow. It was *horrible*! I spit it out. *(Use lots of body language here.)* Boy, then I *really* needed a drink of good water. So I tried it again, and it was sweet and clear.

Now, do you think this really happened? . . . No, it didn't happen, and it can't happen. I just made up the story. You can't get sweet and bitter water out of the same spring. God says so. But — now listen carefully — you can pray very

* **James 3:8-12**

sweetly at night, and then say some very nasty and mean things the next day. And they both come out of the same mouth. *(Open your mouth and point in.)* Of course, we don't want you to stop praying, but God does not want us to praise the Lord out of one side of our mouth, and say something nasty out of the other. Just so you'll know this is what God really said, let's read it in the Bible. *(Read James 3:8-12.)*

#38

WHO ARE THE MOST UNGRATEFUL PEOPLE?*

Ingratitude

Do you kids like riddles? What kind do you like, easy ones or hard ones?

I think this is an easy one, but we'll see. Are you ready? Listen carefully. Who were the most ungrateful people in the Bible? Now, I know you've heard about them in church here, and especially in Sunday school. Who were the most ungrateful people in the Bible? *(Let them think for a few seconds. To the audience:)* No coaching, now!

... Well, maybe I'll give you a clue: there were nine of them. *(Wait.)* Still need another clue? OK, they had leprosy! That's right — they were the nine lepers. Of course, Jesus healed them, but *only one* came back to say thanks. Can you imagine that? Leprosy is a horrible disease. It eats away your flesh. How could anybody be so ungrateful?

Here's another riddle: how many of us got out of bed this morning? That's an easy one, isn't it? All of us, because we are all here. But how many millions of boys and girls are too sick or too crippled to get up? How many of us jumped out of bed *(lots of action here)* and shouted, "Oh, God, thank you that I can get up!"? Did you get enough to eat this morning? Do you know half of the people in the world were still hungry *after* breakfast and will go to bed that same way? Did any of us get up from the table and shout, "Thank you, Lord, for my good breakfast!"? Now, here's one last riddle, and we should be thinking about this answer all week long. Are you ready for it? *Are we any better than those nine lepers?*

* **Luke 17:11-19**

#39

WHO BROUGHT
THAT GUN IN HERE?*

Evil Words

Good morning.

We're going to talk about deadly weapons this morning, and we're going to have a little quiz. Now, even if you aren't much interested in weapons, join in our quiz — you might even win. OK? Now, I want you to name all the deadly weapons you can think of. Start with the one you think is the deadliest. *(Get as many answers as you can, and suggest any not mentioned.)*

Now let's vote. Which do you think is the most deadly of all? *(Get an answer from a show of hands.)* Are you all satisfied that that is the worst one? I'm not. In fact, nobody even mentioned the most dangerous one. This is going to surprise you. Listen carefully.

The most dangerous weapon of all, the thing that causes more damage than anything else in the world . . . each of you brought it into church this morning! That's hard to believe, isn't it? It's true — the Bible says so. You brought in something deadly. It's more dangerous than any weapon of war. It's worse than any deadly disease, and each one of us carries it with him every day. Now . . . what is it? *(If you get no right answer, say:)* Well, let's look in the answer book. *(Read James 3:2-11.)*

Now, what is it? Our tongue! The things we say, the words we say, can really hurt. You can make your friend your enemy, just with your tongue — just with a few mean words. A U.S. president or a Russian dictator could start a war that would kill millions just by saying ten words. You could hit somebody with a stick, and in a few days, he could forget it, but you could say something cruel and mean and nasty, and he might remember it all his life.

We have to be so careful. We carry a dangerous weapon. *(If you add the following, it will somewhat dilute the impact of the former, but it does finish the story on a positive note.)*

* James 3:5-10

But our words can also do good, wonderful things. Today, each one of us should tell somebody we love him or her. It would make that person so happy. We should apologize to someone today. It would make both of us feel good. So you see, we carry with us a dangerous weapon — but also a wonderful tool to bless people with . . .

It all depends on how we use it.

#40

YOU WON'T COME OUT

THE SAME*

Purity of Heart

Good morning.

Does your teacher ever take you on field trips? You know — like going to visit a fire station, or to a factory or a museum? These are lots of fun, aren't they? You can learn a lot that way.

This morning, I'd like to tell you a story about a class that went to visit a coal mine. Anybody want to tell us what coal is? *(Pause.)* Yes, coal is like big chunks of black rock that burn. Some of your great-great-grandparents burned it in a big black stove to cook their dinner, and also to heat their houses.

A mine is a deep hole in the ground where men dig for gold, silver, coal and many kinds of metals. Mines are very dirty inside, but none are as dirty as coal mines. When the miners come up out of the mines at the end of a day's work, their faces are as black as the coal is.

Well, the day before the students were to visit the mine, the teacher said, "Now remember, children, be sure you wear some real old clothes tomorrow, because we will be going into a very black mine, and we would not want you to spoil any of your nice things." Well, when the bus pulled up in front of the coal mine the next day, there was one girl, named Hortense, who didn't pay any attention to what the teacher had said. She had a white frilly party dress that she had gotten for her birthday, and that is what she was wearing. The mine superintendent met them at the gate. He saw

* **Proverbs 6:27**

Hortense's white dress, and he said, "You'd better not wear that white dress in the mine."

But Hortense said *(say this in a snippy, spoiled-brat way)*, "Well, I guess I can wear this white dress in the mine if I want to."

The superintendent said, "Yes, I guess you can wear that *white* dress in, but I'll tell you, little girl, you won't wear a white dress out." And that's just what happened. When she came out, her dress was more black than white.

Solomon, one of the wisest men who ever lived, said, "Do you think you can hold onto fire without getting burned?" Hortense thought she could. She thought she could go into someplace black and still come out white.

All your lives, you kids are going to be tempted to do things, say things, read things, eat things that God and your parents have told you not to. The devil, and sometimes your friends, will say, "Go ahead, it won't hurt you just this once." Don't believe them. Remember this story. Hortense came out of that mine dirty, and your heart gets dirty every time you do, say, hear or read a dirty thing. Sure, you can drink, swear, cheat and steal. But it's like playing with fire: you will get burned.

#41

HEY, I DIDN'T PLANT THAT!*

Bad Habits

Good morning, kids. I wonder, do any of you like to plant flowers? Do you like to watch them grow? *(Go through the motions of each of these processes.)* You put that tiny seed in the ground, give it some water *(make motions like you're using a hose or watering can)*, and then you wait. *(Tap your foot and look impatient.)* Then *look*! A little piece of dirt pops up, and underneath is something green. Each day, it gets bigger and bigger. And then *look*! A little *bud*, and soon a beautiful flower, pops out. Isn't it wonderful how God does it?

What else grows in your garden? *(Wait for answers; if the one you want isn't forthcoming, give a hint, such as,*

* **Psalm 19:7-14**

"something you didn't *plant and* don't *want."*) That's right, weeds. But how can you tell a good plant from a weed? Well, you can't always know for sure, but this is what I found out. If it grows where you don't want it to; if you never have to water it; if you can step on it without hurting it; if it grows best when you don't pay attention to it . . . it's a *weed.*

Now, let's pretend your life is a garden. OK? What would the good things you do be like? . . . That's right, the flowers. OK, if the good things we do, the good habits we have, are the flowers, what are the bad things, the bad habits, like? Right! The weeds. And just like those weeds in your garden, bad habits don't need any care, any attention. They just want you to ignore them, and they will grow bigger and bigger and bigger. *(Your voice should show these growing.)* Did you ever hear anyone say, "I've got to remember to be mean to my sister today."? Oh, no, those bad habits are weeds. They will grow all by themselves.

Now, suppose when you go home for dinner, you find someone you didn't invite, someone you don't like the looks of, sitting at your dinner table. Well, your mom says, "It's OK, we will get rid of him tomorrow." But tomorrow, instead of one, there are *three,* and they don't want to leave! And soon there are *six . . .* then *ten!* Then your whole house is full of them *(horrified look on your face).* They are eating *all your food,* and they won't leave. They hang on like everything if you try to pull them out. *(Clench your fingers together to show weeds gripping.)*

That's just what weeds, bad habits, do in your life. They grow like everything. They get bigger and worse every day. So as soon as you realize, or your mom or dad tells you, that you have a bad habit, do what you have to do with a weed. Pull it out. Stop it. . . . If you don't, *you know what will happen! (This last part is said in a loud whisper.)*

I'm going to tell you a secret. If you soak the ground with water, weeds come up easily. If you don't, they just break off at the top and they will sprout up again . . . and be bigger than the first time. And when you soak your mind and heart by reading the Bible, and by talking to Jesus, then your bad habits will pull out a lot more easily. That's a secret maybe you should tell your mom and dad, too, OK?

#42

SIN LEAVES SCARS*

The Consequences of Sin

(Construct a simple house out of paper; some simple colors for trim, etc., will make it more interesting, although they aren't necessary. Have a small watering can or pitcher filled with water. The house should be placed in the center of a cookie sheet. At the appropriate time, set a match to the paper house and let it burn long enough to be significantly damaged. Then douse the fire with the pitcher of water.)

We all know, I'm sure, that the Bible says that if we confess our sins, God will surely forgive us our sins and make our hearts clean again. This is true. God will surely do it, but I'd like to ask you a question: because God will always forgive us if we confess, does it matter how many times we sin? Do we have to worry about doing bad things because God's going to forgive us if we ask him to? What do you think?

It's true — if we confess and are sorry, God will forgive. But did you know that sin leaves scars sometimes? Now, somebody could steal a motorcycle out of our church parking lot and crash it while he is trying to escape. God will forgive him if he confesses and is sorry, but if he tears his cheek off in the crash, he will have an ugly scar. God won't change that. If you tell lies at school, God will forgive you if you confess, but if the kids all call you *liar,* God won't change that.

Let me show you another way. Let's pretend this is your house. Now your mom has gone to the store and left you there with a friend of yours. You want to show your friend a trick you learned from someone at school. You do it with matches. Now you know your mom has told you many, many times, *"Don't ever play with matches,"* but you think you can be real careful, so you do it anyway. You don't know how it happened, but your house caught fire. *(At this point, ignite it. When you have doused it:)* Doesn't that look terrible? Can God forgive a sin like *this*? *(Pause.)* Yes. But will he turn that burnt house back into a nice house again? No. You see, sin can leave terrible scars. So you want to remember this whenever you're tempted to do anything you know God doesn't like.

* **I John 1:9**

#43

BUT EVERYBODY ELSE

IS DOING IT!*

Standing Up for What's Right

Have you kids ever done anything just because all your friends were doing it, and then you found out it was the wrong thing to do? Have you ever said to your mom or dad, "Well, Suzy *(or Billy or whoever)* was doing it."?

Let me tell you about a little boy who said that once. He did something he really shouldn't have, and his mother was scolding him. He said, "Ah, Mom, all the other kids were doing it."

"Sit down, Georgie," she said, "and let me tell you a story.

"When I was a little girl, we lived on your grandpa's farm. We didn't have people who came to pick up our garbage, so Grandpa dug a big, wide hole at the end of the farm, where he dumped all his trash, garbage, oil, fish heads and lots of yucky stuff like that. He put a fence around the hole to keep the sheep from falling in. But one day, a sheep found a hole in the fence, and he went through and down into the muck. And do you know what? All the other sheep followed him. There they were, all dirty, covered with grease, and crying like babies."

Georgie started to laugh. *(Here, you should laugh heartily, and say — Georgie talking: "Those stupid sheep!" Laugh again, then suddenly let your laughter turn to a sheepish grin.)*

"Georgie," his mom said, "you're not stupid. You're a smart little boy, and I love you; but today you were like those sheep, weren't you?" Georgie had to admit that he was. Then he decided he was hungry, so his mom gave him a cookie.

That's a good story to remember, isn't it, when we start to follow somebody else? Now I hope you're not all hungry, because I don't have any cookies.

---

* **Proverbs 4:13-15 and 14:7**

#44

OUCH! THAT HURTS!*

Self-Control

Did you ever see somebody prune a tree? What is pruning? Can anyone tell me? *(If you don't get a satisfactory answer, briefly explain.)* Why do we have to prune trees? Well, if it's a fruit tree, we prune it so we can get bigger and better fruit. If we don't prune, we'll just get a lot of leaves. Now, leaves are nice, but it's the fruit we like to eat, isn't it?

Suppose your mom said, "How would you like a piece of toast and some nice apricot-leaf jam?" Yuk! It's apricots you want, not the leaves. *(Change the fruit in this example to what is grown in your area — apples, plums, etc.)* And if you want the nice big apricots, you have to prune the tree.

Now suppose your dad got his pruning knife ready, but your sister said, "Oh, I'm sure it's going to hurt the tree when you cut its branches. I don't think we ought to do it." Well, sure it hurts. Pruning always hurts, but it's good for the tree. If you don't shorten some of the tree's branches, they could get too long and too heavy, and a big wind could come along and break them off. So trees need pruning.

Do people need pruning, too? Sure, they do — especially kids. Now, that sounds scary. How do you prune a kid? Well, of course, not by chopping off any branches. *(Hold out your arm to suggest a branch.)* No, kids get pruned when we cut out some of the things that are not good for them. But it's always best if we prune ourselves. Let me show you how pruning yourself works. Suppose you were goofing off in Sunday school. It was kind of fun, but you knew you really shouldn't have been doing it. So you decide you aren't going to do that anymore. *That's* pruning yourself.

Now suppose your mom keeps telling you to turn off the TV and get to your homework. You keep saying, "Ah, Mom, just fifteen minutes more." Finally, she goes over and pushes the button. Off goes the picture. That's pruning. That's good for you, and someday, you'll thank your mom that she didn't let you grow up to be a dummy.

* **John 15:1-3**

But do you know when pruning hurts the most? When God has to do it for you. He wants us to prune ourselves, but if we don't, sometimes he does it, and then it really hurts.

It's not true in every case, of course, but a lot of people feel bad because some habit or appetite didn't get pruned out of their lives. And some people who have unhappy homes didn't pay any attention to what God says about pruning. Just about all the people in jail are there because they wouldn't prune out all the things they were doing that are against the law. Now they are getting pruned, and they really hurt.

Oh, I almost forgot. Do you know what is the best book about pruning ever written? *(Pause.)* Right! The Bible.

#45

TIME TO WASH UP*

Getting Rid of Sin

Do you like to go to bed at night. *(Pause for answers.)* Do you ever say, "Aw, Mom, just ten minutes more?" What don't you like about going to bed? *(Pause.)* It's dark? You don't like putting away your toys? You don't like washing your hands and face, or showering, or brushing your teeth? You know, I've never met a boy or girl who *liked* to get cleaned up. I wonder why. Do boys and girls think it's a waste of soap and water, and they don't like to waste things?

But even if you don't like it, you do know it's very important, don't you? Does your mom stand at the bedroom door and inspect? Does she look at your hands and face and check behind your ears? *(Pantomime these actions.)*

I think somebody else, somebody you can't see, is also watching you. Now, of course, he wants clean hands and a clean face, too, but mostly, he wants to know if you're going to bed with a clean heart. That's a lot more important than clean hands, isn't it?

Maybe you should suggest this to your mom and dad: have *heart clean-up time*! Your mom could say, "OK, it's clean-up time on the inside: Now, did you get mad at anybody

* **Ephesians 4:26**

today? Are you still mad? God says you mustn't go to sleep mad, so forgive whomever you have been mad at. And if it was your fault, ask God to forgive you. OK, that's done. That's clean. Now, anything else? Were you the kind of kid you should have been in school today? Maybe you should talk to God about that. Did you remember to be thankful for everything?"

You know, I think if we did this, we'd be the cleanest kids in the whole wide world.

#46

THE TWO SADDEST WORDS*

The Importance of the Present

Did you ever think of what wonderful things words are? We can do so many things, just with words. You can save a person's life sometime just by shouting *(shout)*, "Look out!" when he is in danger. Or with just three words, *I love you*, you can make so many people happy — your mom, your dad, *especially* your grandma.

There are exciting words, there are happy words, and there are sad words. What are some happy words? *(Pause for answers.)* Now how about sad words? *(Pause.)* Yes, those are sad words, all right, but what do you think are the two saddest words ever spoken? *(Pause.)* Let me give you a couple of clues:

One day you really had to get to school on time, for something special you really wanted to do. But you fooled around eating your breakfast and getting dressed, and then when you ran to the corner to catch the bus, it had just left. *(Show dejection.)* Or your mom was waiting for a big sale on washing machines. Finally, she found one, one hundred dollars off for one day only. She waited until the afternoon to go to town, and when she got to the store, they had just sold the last one. *(Look sad.)* Your dad is hurrying to the airport to catch a plane, but there is a traffic jam on the freeway, and he gets there just in time to see the plane take off without him. *(Show disgust and frustration.)* Now, what are the two words? *(Pause.)* Right! *Too late.*

* **II Corinthians 6:2**

Some of you look as though you don't think th
the two saddest words. Well, let me tell you anothe
It's about a boy who knew he should ask Jesus to co... ....o
his heart. His mom and dad, his Sunday school teacher, and
his pastor had talked to him about it many times. But he
thought, "Someday I will ask him, but if I do that now, it
might spoil some of my fun." Well, one day he was showing
off for some of his friends. He was sitting on the seat of his
bike with his feet on the handlebars, coasting down a hill.
He looked back to see if his friends were watching *(turn and
look back)*, and didn't see a car coming out of a side street.
(Clap your hands together as you shout this:) Smash! He had
intended to ask Jesus to forgive him — someday — to ask
him to come into his heart — someday. But now, at his fu-
eral, it was too late. The two saddest words in our language —
too late. . . . Let's very quietly go back to our seats.

#47

WHY DO I

HAVE TO HURT, LORD?*

Confession

Did any of you kids ever have a toothache? It sure
hurts, doesn't it? How about a stomachache? *(Pause for answers.)* I know some of you have had those. Which is worse,
a toothache or a stomachache? How many think a toothache
is worse? *(Wait for a show of hands.)* How many think a
stomachache is worse? *(Wait for a show of hands.)* One thing
we know for sure: both of them hurt real bad, don't they?

When you're hurting like that, do you ever wish God
wouldn't let people have any pain? Do you think it would
be better if he didn't let things hurt us? Do you know why
God lets it hurt when things happen to our body? *(Pause for
answers.)* He does that to *protect us.* If my stomach didn't
hurt when I was sick, I wouldn't know I was sick, and I
wouldn't go to the doctor, and I might even die. You see,
God sends pain to tell me, "Something is wrong in your body.
Do something about it." Not long ago, I read about a baby
who couldn't feel pain. When she was a year old, she bit off
the end of her finger, and she *didn't even feel it.* So you see
why we need pain.

* **Psalm 32:3**

Did you ever wish you didn't feel so bad in here *(point to your heart)* when you did something you know you shouldn't have done, something you know Jesus doesn't like, something our Bible says is sin? That is your heart's *(point)* pain, your heart hurting. That's God warning you that you need some medicine. Do you know what that medicine is? *(Pause for answers.)* It's confession; it's saying, "I'm sorry I did that bad thing. Forgive me." You see, if you didn't get that heart pain, you'd never ask God to forgive you. And the Bible says that if we don't confess our sin, God will not forgive us and make us clean again. But when we do *(all smiles now)* confess, God takes all that heart pain away, and we feel *so good* again. Isn't it wonderful the way God loves us and does everything so that our hearts and our bodies can be in great shape?

#48

YOU WERE THERE*

Forgiveness for Sins

(If this story is used on Easter Sunday, a reference to the Resurrection should be added.)
You know, kids, I was reading something very interesting the other day. *(Since you are reading it here, you can in truth say this.)* Now we know Jesus was crucified on a terrible Roman cross, but did you know that this was the cruelest kind of punishment anyone ever had to suffer? If you were to give a criminal a choice of being hanged by the neck, or burned at the stake, or crucified, he would never choose crucifixion. It was horrible, but Jesus went through this for us.

I was wondering — have you ever wished you had lived back when Moses crossed the Red Sea? Have you wished you were there when David killed the giant Goliath with one stone? Would you like to have been with those shepherds when they peeked into the manger and saw the baby Jesus? Or would you like to have been in that boat with Jesus and the disciples during that bad storm when Jesus told the wind

* **Luke 23:42-43**

and the waves to calm down — and they did?

How about Mt. Calvary — would you like to have been there when Jesus was crucified? Oh, no! I sure would not want to have been there . . . but *I was*! Yes, and so were you, and so was everyone in this room, even though Jesus was crucified almost two thousand years ago.

Do you remember those two thieves who were crucified with Jesus? Do you remember what they did? One of them shouted insults at Jesus, but the other blamed himself and called Jesus "Lord," and said, "Remember me when you come into your kingdom." So you see, both of them were guilty, just as we are guilty. That's what I mean when I say that we were there, just as those two thieves were there. If we have never asked Jesus to forgive us, if we have never accepted him as our Savior, then we know which thief we are like. But if we have, then we are like that thief who was sorry for his sins. Jesus told that thief — and he tells us — that he would be with Jesus in heaven. So you see, it sure makes a difference which side of the cross we are on, doesn't it?

Now do you see what I meant? We really were there.

HOLIDAYS AND SPECIAL USE

☆ *Special Use: Valentine's Day*
#49

WHO SENT THE FIRST ONE?*

The Greatest Gift

I've got some things behind my back. I'm going to give one to each of you, but first I want you to guess what they are. I'll give you some hints, some clues, but I don't want you to guess, though, until I give you all the clues. OK?

First, someone gave one to many people almost two thousand years ago, and people have been giving them to each other for hundreds of years since. They come in all sizes and shapes. Most of them have written messages on them. Some say real mushy things, especially if you get one from your sweetheart.

Now, what do I have behind my back? Right! Valentines. And I've got one for each of you.

Who gave the first valentine? *(If you don't get the right answer, say:)* I'll give you another clue: it didn't come in a box or an envelope. The world's first valentine came in a manger.

Now, who gave us the first valentine? God did, didn't he? Jesus is God's valentine to us. It was God's way of saying, "I love you." Wouldn't it be wonderful if we could send a valentine back to God? I think we can send one, and just the one God wants — the one he asked for. In the Bible, God said, "Son, daughter, give me your heart." So you see, we can give God a valentine — the best one anyone can give.

* Proverbs 23:26

☆ *Special Use: Mother's/Father's Day*
#50

GOD, I DID WRONG!*

Forgiveness

Good morning, children.

Who can tell me what special day this is? Of course, we all know it's Mother's Day *(or Father's Day)*. This is the day we want to remember our moms *(or dads)* in a special way and let them know how much we love them. I know you are all very thankful for your mom *(or dad)* for a lot of reasons, but let's see if we can find out what some of them are. When I point to you, I'd like you to finish this statement: "I'm thankful for my mom *(or dad)* because — ." For instance, you could say something like, "Because she *(or he)* always reads me stories," or, "She *(or he)* always has a treat for me when I get home from school." OK, are you ready? *(Get as many answers as time will permit. Make some appropriate remarks such as, "Yes, mothers/fathers are always doing wonderful things for us," etc.)*

Thank you for telling us all that, but do you know something I noticed? None of you said you were thankful because your mom *(or dad)* punished you in some way when you did something you shouldn't have done. Now why do you suppose that was? We don't like to be scolded or punished, do we? We don't like to be corrected, but we all need to be sometimes — even our moms and dads — because it's good for us. God said so. In the Bible *(Hebrews 12:11)*, God says that being punished isn't much fun while it's happening, but afterward, we can see how much good it did us. Sometimes being punished is the only way we learn how to do things that are good for ourselves and everyone around us.

Let me tell you a story about two kings who were really scolded by God, and about what they did when God punished them.

The first one was King David. He was a good king. You remember, when he was a shepherd boy, he killed the giant Goliath by knocking him out with a sling and then cutting his head off. David *loved* God, and God made him very rich and very popular. It was David who wrote most of the book of Psalms in the Bible.

---

* Hebrews 12:11

But one day, David saw a beautiful woman named Bathsheba. David wanted her for *his* wife, so he put her soldier husband at a dangerous place where he was sure to be killed, and that's just what happened. God was very angry over David's terrible sin, and told the prophet Nathan to tell David how he was going to be punished for his awful sin. *(Say these next few lines using the whining tone that children use when they are trying to excuse themselves.)* Now, David could have said, "I couldn't help it. . . . I didn't mean to. . . . It wasn't my fault . . ." But he didn't. "No," David confessed, "it was all my fault. I sinned against you, Lord." David was punished very severely, but God forgave him, and David loved God all the more.

Now let's look at another king. He was David's great-great-grandson. His name was Asa. Asa also was a good king. He tore down all the idols and altars where people were worshipping false gods, and God rescued him and his people from enemies who were much bigger and stronger than they were.

One day, King Asa found out that another king and his army were coming to fight them. But instead of asking God to help him, he paid money to get a bad king to come and help him fight his war. Again God was angry, and he sent another prophet to tell Asa, "Because you did this, now you really are going to have war, and I won't help you." Asa was so furious that he threw the prophet in jail. King Asa didn't confess to God as King David had, and very soon Asa got sick and died.

You see, both kings sinned, but David said, "God, I'm wrong. Forgive me." And God did forgive him. God didn't forgive Asa, because Asa did not say he was sorry; he just got mad.

David's son Solomon wrote these words in the Bible: "Young man, do not resent it when God chastens and corrects you, for his punishment is proof of his love." And that's also true when your mother *(or father)* punishes you. It's because she *(or he)* loves you enough to try to teach you what is best for you.

☆ *Special Use: Thanksgiving*
#51

BUT I DON'T LIKE THAT STUFF*

Thankfulness

Good morning, kids.

I'm going to find out something this morning. When I point to you, I want you to quickly tell me what you had for breakfast. OK? *(Get as many answers as time will reasonably allow.)*

Now, did you all get enough to eat? Did you like what you had? Did some of you want some sugar-frosted cereal with sugar and cream on top instead of what you had? How about blueberry waffles smothered in strawberry jam . . . cocoa with two big, fat, juicy marshmallows melting on top . . . or maybe you would have liked a big pile of pancakes drowning in syrup, with a ring of smoked links all around. *(This is all smiles.)*

Did you know *(this is serious)* that half of the kids in the world didn't get enough to eat this morning? And do you know what else? They will be very hungry when they go to bed tonight.

I saw you all come running into Sunday school. The door was wide open. Five hundred kids could have come in with you. There are places in the world where you could be arrested if you did that.

How are you all feeling? You all look great. *(To a boy)* _____ , make a muscle. *(Show him how if he doesn't understand, or show him ahead of time. Then feel his muscle.)* Wow! Just like a band of steel. Isn't it wonderful to be healthy and strong?

But there are thousands and thousands of boys and girls just like you who are in the hospital today . . . some with broken bodies. . . . Some are never going to come out alive.

Now why are we telling you this? Just to make you feel bad? Just to spoil your fun? *No!* But just so that you, and your mommy and your daddy, and all of the people in our church, will realize that we are the most richly blessed people on this earth. So each of us should remember to thank God many times a day for everything he has given us.

* Psalm 118:1

☆ *Special Use: Christmas*

#52

A MOST UNUSUAL PARTY*

Living for Jesus

Do you like birthday parties? *(Pause for answers.)* What do you like about them? Oh, sure, we all like to get presents. Even when you're older, you like to have people remember you, and parties are always fun.

Now I'm going to tell you a story about a special birthday party, and when I'm done, I want you to tell me if it's true.

It was a very unusual party. There were lots of people who came. In fact, by the time the guest of honor came, there was no room for him at all. The people there said, "You'll have to go out in the barn; there is no room for you here." And so that's what he did.

Many years passed, and people began to think that it was too bad that there had been no room for him, so they decided to have a party for him every year. And of course, they brought presents — lots of them. And every year, the party got bigger and bigger, and people brought more and more gifts — millions of them. But do you know a very strange thing? Not one of those presents was for the one whose birthday it was. Everybody else got presents but him.

Tell me, is this a true story? *(Wait for answers.)* Yes, it's true, isn't it? Everybody gets presents on Jesus' birthday except Jesus.

Suppose on Christmas your mom tied a big ribbon on your old bike, or wrapped up one of your dolls for you as a Christmas present. You'd say, "Hey, that was mine already." And that would be true. So how can we give Jesus a present? Everything already belongs to him. Well, we can tell him, and mean it, that we want to live for him. That's the gift he wants, and the best one we could ever give.

* **Luke 2:6-7**

ABOUT THE AUTHOR

Ted Lazicki has had a ministry of writing children's stories and plays over a 30-year time span — this while serving as Sunday school teacher, superintendent and church elder.

Several of his plays have been published, and many of his stories and articles have appeared in his denomination's (Church of the Lutheran Brethren) periodicals. Retired now from his secular position, he lives with his wife Fern in Arcadia, California, on his Lazy Z Ranch (a huge half-acre spread which mysteriously swells to five acres every time the grass needs mowing).

Of his six children, one son is a missionary in Cameroon, Africa; another, a pastor in Eugene, Oregon. One daughter has a ministry to Chinese and Vietnamese refugees in Pasadena, California, and two others are pastors' wives in Pennsylvania and Arizona. The youngest daughter is in college.

"I spend my days," Ted says, "reading, writing and repairing, with a totally disproportionate amount of time spent on the latter. We hike in California's high Sierras, and visit our far-flung children as often as funds and our consciences will permit us."

Notes:

Notes:

Ted Lazicki's first book of children's sermons, SOMETHING FOR THE KIDS, was so popular that Christian educators clamored for more! You'll be delighted by these friendly chats with children — another year's worth — in this follow-up book:

WHERE DOES GOD LIVE?

by

TED LAZICKI

When you see those little upturned faces looking at you expectantly, you want to give them a message that is fun to listen to and easily understood — without exceeding their attention span. This book offers 58 story-sermons written in a fresh, enthusiastic style. You won't be preaching to them, but rather talking to them friend-to-friend — and they'll respond beautifully!

Sample titles include:

"Watch Out for That Bulldozer!" (Building Godly Lives)

"You Gotta Have a Reservation" (Heaven)

"It's a Talking Book — Really!" (The Bible)

"Look — My Hands Can Say I Love You!" (Service)

You'll never be at a loss when it's time for the children's sermon again with these lively ideas!

ORDER FORM

MERIWETHER PUBLISHING LTD.
P.O. BOX 7710
COLORADO SPRINGS, CO 80933
TELEPHONE: (719) 594-4422

Please send me the following books:

————— **Something for the Kids #CC-B192** $9.95
by Ted Lazicki
Fifty-two "front-row" sermons for children

————— **Where Does God Live? #CC-B189** $9.95
by Ted Lazicki
Fifty-eight children's sermons for worship

————— **Teaching With Bible Games #CC-B108** $10.95
by Ed Dunlop
20 "kid-tested" contests for Christian education

————— **Let's Play a Bible Game! #CC-B183** $12.95
by Ed Dunlop
Scripture puzzles and games for overhead projectors

————— **The Official Sunday School Teachers** $9.95
Handbook #CC-B152
by Joanne Owens
An indispensable aid for anyone involved in Sunday school activities

————— **Storytelling From the Bible #CC-B145** $10.95
by Janet Litherland
The art of biblical storytelling

————— **Costuming the Christmas and Easter** $9.95
Play #CC-B180
by Alice M. Staeheli
How to costume any religious play

These and other fine Meriwether Publishing books are available at your local Christian bookstore or direct from the publisher. Use the handy order form on this page.

NAME: _____

ORGANIZATION NAME: _____

ADDRESS: _____

CITY:_____ STATE: _____ ZIP: _____

PHONE: _____

❑ **Check Enclosed**
❑ **Visa or MasterCard #** _____

Signature: _____   Expiration
　　　　　(required for Visa/MasterCard orders)   Date: _____

COLORADO RESIDENTS: Please add 3% sales tax.
SHIPPING: Include $2.75 for the first book and 50¢ for each additional book ordered.

❑ *Please send me a copy of your complete catalog of books and plays.*